PSYCHOLOGY

CONQUER THE BATTLES OF YOUR MIND WITH POWERFUL TECHNIQUES TO OVERCOME STRESS, ANXIETY & NEGATIVE THINKING

SCOTT COLTER

TABLE OF CONTENTS

FREE GIFT

Drop the Fat Now!
Natural Solutions to Getting Trim

INTRODUCTION

Welcome to this book, Psychology: Conquer the battles of your mind with powerful techniques to overcome stress, anxiety & negative thinking.

Mental health is rapidly becoming an acceptable topic to talk about. Previously, mental health issues were largely swept under the rug by society, due to their inconvenient nature. It can be hard for anyone who hasn't suffered from a mental illness to empathize with someone who has, as mental illness tends to be subtle and obscure.

If someone breaks a bone, demonstrates a high fever, or has a wound to display, it is readily apparent for all too see that they ill or injured. Yet if someone is depressed or anxious, it is unfortunately all too easy to disregard these problems.

However, the climate of mental health issues is gradually and inevitably changing. The fear and stigmatization over mental health and mental health problems is slowly subsiding as people realize that they are too important to be ignored.

It is starting to be appreciated that looking after your mental health is just as critical (if not more so) than bodily health. A keen interest in your mind and your thought patterns is not just sensible, but pro-active and very wise. Every single person on this planet can improve their mental health to be happier and more productive. Whether you have a mental health illness or not, there are bound to be psychological techniques and methods you can use to make yourself content and more fulfilled.

This book aims to help you deal with three aspects of mental health; stress, anxiety and negative thinking. Each of these three harmful states of mind can range in intensity from a mild annoyance to severe condition. Likewise all have the potential to cause and contribute to other mental health problems, such as depression.

This book will give you a thorough insight into how each of these terms should be understood and what you can do to improve them. If you experience stress, anxiety or negative thinking or suspect that someone you know does, there is no need to suffer in silence. Use the knowledge compiled and offered in this book to help yourself and those around you.

There are three chapters in this book;

Managing Stress

Overcoming Anxiety

Conquering Negative Thinking

I hope they can aid you in your quest for happiness and peace of mind.

Managing Stress

Stress is the sensation of being overwhelmed by responsibilities or pressure. As a psychological concept, stress was first introduced in the 1950's, with the term originally taken from physics, where it described the amount of tension placed upon an object.

The important part of the stress definition is *feeling overwhelmed.* Many people have huge levels of responsibility but nonetheless thrive in difficult or taxing situations. Stress is the distinct feeling of being pushed or pulled too thin and it doesn't directly correlate to the level of responsibility that you may have, although responsibility and pressure are often factors.

Stress has a huge range of symptoms. It is known that it can increase blood pressure and heart rate, affect sleeping patterns, produce a loss of appetite, destroy concentration and contribute to a wide range of mental illnesses, such as depression.

When a person feels a sensation of stress, the body's hormonal system kicks into action. The nervous system releases a cocktail of hormones, most notably cortisol, which collectively trigger the 'flight or fight' response.

To simplify, the flight or fight response is an evolution adaptation that prepares the body to either combat a threat ('fight') or run away ('flight'). Ultimately this causes the heart rate to increase, the breath to become faster as well as a redirection of blood flow towards the muscles. More severe effects include shaking, loss of peripheral vision and the constriction of blood vessels. All of these responses are intended to prime the body for dealing with threats or challenges.

Whilst the fight or flight system is a fantastic adaptation that helped our ancestors cope with a harsh and dangerous world, it causes us a range of problems in modern society.

The vast majority of us are not going to need to fight to the death or run away from an apex predator when we experience a stressor. Rather our challenges are commonplace but chronic; a lack of money, workplace issues, interpersonal relationship strains, other desires and aspirations, etc.

The issue is that our flight and fight response can trigger in reaction to these mundane, but non-life threatening issues. If this response triggers too frequently, a high amount of flight & fight hormones are released, especially cortisol, into the body, producing the psychological sensation of stress.

Once you begin to understand that stress is a *response*, the methods in which stress can be tackled start to become clear – recognize what is causing the stress response and manage that.

Anything that causes a stress response is called a *stressor.* The crucial part of stressors is that they can be divided into *physiological* stressors and *psychological* stressors.

Physiological stressors are events that directly put pressure upon the body, such as injury or extreme environmental temperatures.

Psychological stressors, however, are any events that are *perceived* as threatening or challenging. Depending upon the individual, this may include genuinely dangerous events (such as being mugged or attacked) to events that are actually harmless (such as an offhand comment interpreted negatively).

Therefore to manage stress, you need to analyze both your proximity to stressors and your perception of them. It may be the case that you have too many stressors within your life, in which case you need to cut back on events that are causing you stress.

However, it may be that you are interpreting too many manageable events as stressors, in which case you need to alter the ways you are perceiving these events.

Additionally, stress can also be managed by adopting a healthier lifestyle, which can manage the physiological causes and symptoms of stress. Let us walk through each of these solutions to stress in turn.

RECOGNIZING STRESS

Regardless of whether your stress problem arises from the fact that you are experiencing too many stressors or that your perception of them is too negative, the first step is recognizing what stressors you have.

One of the best ways to achieve this is to keep a daily journal of each time during the day that you have felt under considerable stress. It is best if you keep this journal as detailed as possible, detailing not just the date, but also the exact time you were feeling stressed, the intensity of the stress sensation and relevant details such as the people you were with or what activities you were doing.

If you manage to keep a journal persistently you will likely realize certain patterns of stress. It may be the case that interactions with a particular person you are finding especially stressful, for example.

In addition to keeping a journal, engaging in mindfulness is a potent stress-reduction technique. Mindfulness is increasingly sought as an antidote to the sensation of stress itself, but it is also useful for increasing your recognition of stressors. The more mindful you are of your day-to-day life, the higher chance you intimately realize the circumstances where you feel stressed (and therefore have a better chance at interpreting/managing these circumstances).

Mindfulness as a topic will be covered under the negative thinking chapter later in this book. Nonetheless be aware that the instructions and advice regarding mindfulness in that chapter can also be applied for stress reduction.

On a similar vein, it is important to understand what habits you have that may be coping mechanisms for the stress you are experiencing. Not all coping mechanisms are classified as unhealthy, but many are. Common coping methods include smoking, drinking, drug usage or anger venting. Ensure that you don't trade one evil – stress – for another. Learn to recognize your reactions to situations to analyze whether your unhealthy tendencies are indeed a reaction to your stress.

CHANGING STRESSOR PERCEPTION – COGNITIVE BEHAVIORAL THERAPY

Cognitive behavioral therapy (or CBT for short) is one of the predominant therapies for dealing with a myriad of cognitive problems and mental health issues, including stress, anxiety and negative thinking. Therefore when you read those later chapters, bear this section on CBT in mind.

CBT is based upon the cognitive approach in psychology. To simplify, the cognitive approach is a framework that claims that thoughts ("cognitions") drive behavior. Therefore if you want to change your behavior, you must look at the underlying thought patterns that drive that behavior and change those. Hence, cognitive-behavioral therapy as the name for the application of this theory.

CBT is usually done with a trained therapist who helps you systematically and logically identify your thought patterns and transform them into more productive and successful alternatives.

Nonetheless, there are many resources and guides detailing the method and techniques CBT uses, which you can employ by yourself. Try reading an introductory book on the topic of CBT to see if you can change your perception of stressors, especially those which you cannot avoid or otherwise manage.

Healthier Lifestyle

It is easy to think of a 'healthy' lifestyle as purely a physical term, but it includes our habits that may produce positive or negative states of mind. There are a myriad of ways you can improve your lifestyle, which can indirectly lower the feelings of stress you may be experiencing.

The first and most common lifestyle habit is to exercise regularly. Exercise is defined as any type of activity that is exerting enough to produce an increase in heart rate and produce sweating. Therefore exercise isn't just limited to the gym or sports center but also ordinary activities, such as walking or housework, as long as these activities are of an appropriate intensity. It is recommended by most health authorities to exercise for at least

150 minutes every week, yet most of us receive notably less levels of exercise than this.

Exercise releases endorphins, which are your body's pleasure chemicals. The positive sensation can psychologically counteract the negative sensation of stress, but the benefits of exercise on stress relief may be more subtle. Exercise improves cognitive function, makes it easier to sleep and increases alertness and mindfulness. It is likely that each of these factors also contribute to the decreased levels of stress frequent exercisers experience.

TIME MANAGEMENT TECHNIQUES

Another lifestyle technique is to manage your time more effectively. As stress is the result of feelings overburdened and overwhelmed by responsibilities and pressures, learning how to better organize your time can help you achieve more and thus reduce the level of pressure you experience.

The initial step in learning how to improve your time management is to decide upon the goals with which you want to achieve. Start by making a list of advancements which you want to achieve – interpersonal goals, career goals, weight loss, a healthier lifestyle, hobby practice and so on. Prioritize each of these goals depending on how important they are to you.

You may realize that you have been feeling stressed, or devoting a disproportionate amount of time towards goals that are, in fact, not as important to you as you originally perceived. If you have several goals, consider whether it would be best to short-list your goals and tackle the goals you consider most pertinent first.

In addition to goal setting, list making is another common time management technique. All this involves is simply writing down a to-do list of all your current responsibilities. Poor time management is often the result of failing to organize, due to either forgetting about the existence of responsibilities or not prioritizing the most pressing responsibilities. Writing a list is often all that is needed to prevent either of these mishaps from occurring.

One prioritizing technique is to divide all your tasks into the four following types:

1) Urgent & Important

2) Not urgent but important

3) Urgent, but not important

3) Neither urgent or important

Naturally, once categorized as such, it becomes clear to focus on achieving urgent & important tasks first, than tasks that are either urgent or important, but not both simultaneously. Tasks that are neither urgent nor important can be left to last.

SOCIAL CONNECTIONS

In addition to proper time management, another stress reduction is social support and connection. Humans are social animals and as a general law, we are most successful and happiest when we feel connected and appreciated by those who are around us.

Often stress can make us feel like we should isolate ourselves from others; instead it is often wisest to counteract this urge and spend more time with people. Try to organize or capitalize on situations where you can spend time with close friends or family and tell them about what is making you feel stressed.

HELPING OTHERS

Another stress reduction technique involves helping other people through charity, community work or even simple good-deeds to the people around you. People who regularly engage in helping behaviors tend to be happier as well as more resilient to stress. This is due to the fact that helping other people not only makes ourselves feel better, but it also makes us aware of the serious and taxing problems other people face. Whilst this isn't a cause for happiness in itself, it tends to make personal problems feel more tame and manageable.

Likewise, setting some time aside for yourself is another way to reduce stress. It is easy to become obsessed with goal-setting and achievement, pushing ourselves to go further and do more, forgetting the fact that we all need a little 'me time' occasionally.

The problem, as in most things, is achieving the correct balance. Part of the solution to allocating enough downtime is to use the time management techniques before mentioned. Similarly, another popular technique is deciding upon one or two days per week, which after work, are purely relaxation and enjoyment days. The power of strictly deciding one or two days per week where you allow yourself to relax is that you can enjoy that relaxation guilt-free.

Conversely, many people who try to mix in relaxation time between the times allocated for goal-setting and achievement struggle to enjoy the former, without feeling that they should be doing something productive. Rest and relaxation is productive – in moderation!

Overcoming Anxiety

Anxiety is a feeling of worry, trepidation or fear which ranges in intensity, from merely uncomfortable to emotionally crippling. Anxiety is a normal human emotion in response to events where the outcome is important, but unknown. However, many people suffer from the feeling of anxiety in response to everyday events that others would not consider anxiety-inducing, leading to disproportionate levels of anxiety.

Anxiety is a symptom and cause of numerous other mental health problems, such as panic attacks, phobias and social anxiety. However, anxiety can be recognized as a condition on its own, which is termed generalized anxiety disorder. This chapter deals with recognizing the signs and symptoms of anxiety and managing them.

The distinction between generalized anxiety disorder and regular anxiety is characterized by the rational basis of the anxiety felt, it's frequency as well as its impact on the everyday functioning of the person involved. For example, it is considered normal to feel anxious when sitting an important exam for college or waiting in a hospital for the results of an important medical exam.

However, feeling anxious about leaving the house or going to work are, in the majority of cases, unfounded and irrational anxiety responses. Furthermore, feeling anxious whenever you leave the house or go to work will impact the regular day-to-day activities of the individual with anxiety, therefore making a diagnosis of generalized anxiety disorder more appropriate.

Regardless of whether anxiety is experienced as a sensation or as a mental health problem, it can be tackled and reduced through various methods.

HEALTHY LIFESTYLE

The first of these methods is to adopt a healthy lifestyle. Although there may be other factors involved, the physiological experience of anxiety may be triggered or influenced by a variety of physical and emotional factors related to how you live.

Poor sleep hygiene and sleep deprivation can lead to a greater frequency of negative thoughts, which can develop into anxiety or worsen the condition. Various stimulants such as nicotine, sugar, alcohol and caffeine can also induce bodily stress and exertion, which too can make an individual more susceptible to anxiety and panic attacks.

Similarly, the endorphins released during exercise can combat feelings of anxiety and reduce the physiological contributors.

Breathing Techniques

During episodes of anxiety, or panic attacks, the breath can start to become shallow and fast. This is because in a similar manner to our stress response, anxiety can trigger our body's fight or flight response. In fact, panic attacks (commonly associated with anxiety) are interpreted as a strong fight or flight response unconsciously triggered, without an appropriate stimulus.

What distinguishes a panic attack from a regular fight or flight response is that the person who experiences the response starts to panic, focusing their attention upon the bodily sensations, tensing the body and releasing adrenaline which intensifies the symptoms.

Nonetheless, one of the fight or flight responses is to prepare the lungs for more activity – hence rapid, but shallow breaths. Owing to this, it is important to learn breathing techniques that allow yourself to breathe deeply and calmly, to counteract this effect. Furthermore, deep breathing techniques are a fantastic relaxation method, which can give you a calmer mind, helping you tackle your anxieties more directly.

To practice deep breathing, find time during your day where you know you will not be interrupted. Ensure that you are wearing loose clothing so that your breathing rhythms will not be obstructed. Finally, also try to make the area as quiet as possible. This involves selecting a calm period of the day (such as early morning or late evening) where the sounds of the day have passed, but also reducing ambient noise by turning off electrical devices.

Rest in a comfortable position. This may involve lying flat in a bed (or on the floor), sitting in a firm but comfortable chair or sitting cross legged. It is important that you are comfortable, but it is also necessary that you stay awake. If you suspect you might drift off, than it is best to sit in a chair as opposed to lying down.

With this preparation finalized, you can now start to focus upon the breathing. The key to deep breathing is to breathe from the diaphragm (lower stomach) rather than the chest. When you are breathing deeply, you should be able to rest your hand on your navel and feel that area expand and contract as you inhale and exhale.

Start by breathing in, slowly, through your nose, to your lungs maximum capacity – inhale, until you cannot breathe in any further.

Then, gently, exhale, through your mouth, releasing all air until your lungs are empty.

It is best if you breathe in and outwards in conjunction with a number count. As you breathe in, count 1...2...3 than count 1...2...3 as you exhale.

Continue breathing until you start to feel relaxed. If you struggle from anxiety (or if you struggle to relax) you should practice this breathing technique daily, for at least five minutes.

Do not panic or worry if feelings of calmness and relaxation do not immediately arise. For people who are feeling stressed or anxious, the breath may 'catch' or struggle to flow gently. However, if you continue with focused, controlled breathing this tendency will gradually dissipate and the breathing should become pleasant.

This manner of controlled relaxed breathing can also be used in situation where you are feeling anxious. Although it is unlikely that you can sit down and turn off all surrounding distractions, you can still take opportunistic 3-5 minute periods during your day to breathe and calm yourself.

MUSCLE RELAXATION TECHNIQUE

A similar technique to the breathing technique, is the muscle relaxation technique which is designed to help you relax. As you practice the technique over the course of days, weeks and months the prolonged relaxation you experience gradually helps you combat anxiety.

The muscle relaxation technique takes longer than the breathing technique; you will need at least 15-20 minutes of solitude and quiet to practice. As with the breathing technique, make sure you have reduced any ambient noise so you can concentrate fully.

Start by sitting or lying down comfortably and practicing a few moments of deep breathing to rouse your attention. Next, direct your attention towards your left foot. Stretch your foot by contracting and relaxing its muscles. Hold the muscle contraction for 3-5 seconds before release. Keep your awareness on the sensations that arise. Then relax the muscles in your foot and focus on the sensation for a small moment.

Move upwards onto your left calf and stretch and relax this muscle too. Continue working upwards to the thigh, abdomen, shoulder, neck and facial muscles, contracting and relaxing each of these muscles in turn.

When you have reached the crown of the head, work your way down the right side of your body, progressively contracting and releasing the muscles in your face all the way down to your right foot. Ensure that your attention remains focused on each muscle as it contracts and relaxes.

After you have finished the progressive muscle relaxation, spend a few moments lying or sitting with your eyes closed, experiencing any sensations that arise within your body. Once you feel like it is appropriate to do so, gently rise and finish.

It is important to note that it may require several periods of muscle relaxation before the sensation of deep relaxation arises. Therefore it is important to try and practice this technique at least 2-3 times a week (preferably every day).

REDIRECTING ATTENTION

Another anxiety reduction technique is to redirect your attention away from anxious thoughts. This sounds intuitive, but it is generally considered that anxiety suffers experience their symptoms partially due to an inability to redirect attention away from the anxiety/negative thinking patterns and towards other stimuli.

When you next feel anxiety, instead of focusing upon your thoughts and feelings as the anxiety occurs, try to focus on a stimulus in your surroundings. This could be potentially anything, although positively-associated stimuli are more successful. Try to direct more of your attention towards your work, or even a particularly strong, capturing image or sound (such as flower or music).

Similarly, it is important not to over-analyze or interpret your anxiety too deeply. Many anxiety sufferers struggle from the fact that they interpret their anxiety as indicative of the situation at hand. To clarify with an example, if someone feels anxious about their performance at work or school, they may interpret that anxiety as a signal that they are failing or unable to cope with the situation. If they dwell on this interpretation of their anxiety, these people often become paralyzed or experience greater difficulty when encountering these situations in the future.

ANXIETY 'PERIOD'

To people with generalized anxiety disorder, or chronic anxiety suffers in general, it can be hard to cope with the dissonance between what they feel and how much other people tell them to relax and redirect their focus.

To solve this issue and provide a compromise between the need to worry and process anxiety and the need to function some anxiety sufferers have adopted the anxiety 'period'.

This period is a designated time during the day or week (depending on how often a sufferer feels they need it) where you allow yourself to be anxious. For one or two hours you simply allow your worries and fears to be present, without trying to push them away. During this time you consider and reflect upon your anxieties in whatever way you feel appropriate. The strength of the 'anxiety period' is that it allows you to be anxious without feeling any guilt or need to improve yourself.

The anxiety period only works, however, if you postpone and delay all your anxious thoughts and feelings during the day. If an anxious thought occurs during the day, you must tell yourself that you will ponder and reflect on the thought during your anxiety period and then continue with whatever you were doing.

It can be beneficial to write down your worries, as they occur, in a list. This way you can ensure you process and tackle all the anxieties that have manifested themselves during the day.

Creating an anxiety period helps you deal with your life, moment-by-moment, without constantly being distracted by anxieties during the day.

Furthermore, by deliberating creating a space and time to ponder your anxieties, you can often approach them in a calmer, more systematic way than during the moment when they occur. Finally by developing the discipline and skill to postpone your anxieties to a later date, it also helps you discover that you actually have more control over your thoughts and feelings than you might at first have anticipated.

Worst Result Contemplation

Anxiety often arise due to the fear or expectation that a negative outcome to an event or circumstance will arise. For example if you are anxious because you have to give a presentation, you are likely anxious because you are afraid you might stutter or embarrass yourself during the presentation (or some other mishap).

Perhaps counter-intuitively some anxiety suffers can manage their anxiety by contemplating the worst possible outcome to the event or circumstance they may be anxious about. In the overwhelming majority of cases, the level of anxiety felt is disproportionate to the actual worse possible outcome that could occur. For example in the presentation scenario, even if you do embarrass yourself, this is hardly something to be genuinely concerned about.

Most people in the audience will likely sympathize, having been or felt the same from their own experiences. Similarly, most people will forget or not be paying enough attention to the presentation for any embarrassment you feel to even be memorable.

Even if the presentation affects your grades or workplace, you will likely have other opportunities and ways to achieve success, show competence and compensate for a poor presentation.

Ultimately, by following your anxiety to the worst feasible situation that can occur, you can actually calm yourself. By realizing that the worst possible situation is in fact, rather tame, you can approach whatever problem you are facing with a renewed vigor.

Exposure

Anxiety tends to promote avoidance behaviors. If we are anxious about something, it is typical to try and avoid the situation or event that causes this anxiety, unless we have to. For people who experience anxiety relatively infrequently, or people whose circumstances force themselves to tackle their anxieties, this doesn't necessarily pose a problem.

However, for chronic anxiety suffers, you simply cannot flourish in life if you avoid and back down all circumstances and events that make you feel anxious. Rather, you need to slowly expose yourself to these situations and events to learn how to gradually deal with them.

There is no need to plunge yourself in the deep end however. If you have several anxieties, make a list of your anxieties and all the actions and events relating to them. Order the actions and events from what makes you feel least anxious to what makes you feel most anxious.

By doing this, you have provided a repertoire of activities to perform, to acclimatize yourself to anxiety. Start by attempting or doing the activities that make you least anxious (which you are not currently doing).

See if you can do 2-3 of these activities per week. Then, upon successful completion of these activities, you can work your way upon to the activities that make you feel more anxious. Week-by-week, one step at a time, you can climb all the way up to the activities that cause you to feel the most anxious. Over the course of completing these activities, you will grow in confidence and eventually come to terms with the anxieties you feel, causing them to tangibly dissolve.

Even if your anxiety stems around just one particular action or event, see if you can gradually acclimatize yourself to this anxiety. Using the before mentioned example, perhaps you are aware that you are afraid of public speaking. Joining a public speaking group and taking it upon yourself to slowly find opportunities to speak publicly is one the best ways to directly tackle this fear, on your own terms.

ACCEPT IMPERFECTION

Anxiety often arises due to unrealistic expectations that a person may hold themselves to. An anxious person often feels the need to not just succeed, but have an outstanding success. Similarly, any flaw or mishap is interpreted a severe failure.

Conversely, confident and successful people accommodate flaws and mistakes in their lives. Using the on-going pubic speaking example, the best public speakers know how to turn mistakes they make during their speech or presentation into assets, often by improvising around these mistakes or using them as an opportunity to introduce humor.

Likewise, good orators don't allow these mistakes to get in the way of their overall presentation or message – they anticipate they may occur, and accept them when they do. No-one is perfect, so allow yourself your own mistakes and mishaps. If you endorse a realistic standard, you will not get hung up over

mistakes that will inevitably happen in your life.

Conquering Negative Thinking

Negative thinking is an umbrella term for an array of cognitive behaviors that can be interpreted as non-beneficial. Negative thinking is often colloquially interpreted as thoughts that are negative, such as focusing upon failures, short-comings or negative emotions.

However the term can also include other types of thinking, such as intrusive thoughts (thoughts that occur without the desire to do so). Negative thinking is occasionally associated with the term 'cognitive distortions' which describes thinking patterns that inaccurately reflect reality (typically with a negative implication).

This chapter will deal with types of negative thinking and solutions to manage them.

Recognizing Negative Thinking

The essence of negative thinking management is recognizing when negative thoughts are occurring and then counterbalancing negative thoughts with more realistic or positive thinking habits.

The problem with this solution is that people who have a negative thinking tendencies tend to be ignorant about their own thinking patterns. They may realize that they think negatively, but be unaware of how this negative thinking actually manifests (beyond a generalized pessimism). Even more extreme, many negative thinkers fail to recognize that they are in fact guilty of negative thinking to begin with. These individuals tend to interpret their negative thoughts as being accurate and may either think that their thought patterns are the same as everyone else's, or that everyone else is seeing the world through rose-colored glasses.

Therefore, the following section will cover several types of cognitive distortions, with a focus on how these cognitive distortions interplay with negative thinking habits. The result of this exploration should allow you to recognize these patterns of negative thinking, should they occur in yourself or someone you know.

ALL OR NOTHING THINKING

This is a tendency to think of things in absolutes. Situations or events must be entirely positive or entirely negative; there are no ambiguous or mixed cases. However, rarely in life are circumstances so dichotomous.

As most situations or events have positive and negative aspects, all or nothing thinking tends to produce a disproportionate amount of events/situations that are interpreted as negative.

All or nothing thinking therefore often worsens negative thinking patterns and may be a factor in developing depression.

To overcome all or nothing thinking, consider your evaluations of the world around you with more nuance. For example if you commonly have thoughts such as 'I fail at everything I do' or 'everything around me is bad' then you may be guilty of all or nothing thinking. No-one fails at *everything* they do and nor do people experience situations where all things are bad.

It is important to counterbalance all or nothing thoughts with a more realistic interpretation. For example, in the previous two circumstances, a more balanced thought pattern would involve reinforcing and remembering events where you succeed or the enjoyable aspects of life.

OVER-GENERALIZATION

This negative thinking pattern is the tendency to develop a generalization from limited, and often faulty, evidence. A person who overgeneralizes might think a person is a bad person based on one meeting, or that they may never enjoy a new experience if the first time they try it, they don't enjoy it.

Above and beyond the logical fallacy that over-generalization often entails, it also typically results in a greater level of negative interpretation, especially for people who are susceptible to anxiety or depression.

LABELING

This tendency is similar to over-generalization. Labeling is the habit of applying labels to people, rather than interpreting events or actions as temporary or external. For example, if someone is not particularly talkative, a 'labeler' may interpret that person as boring or introverted rather than interpreting that they are not feeling well or that they are tired.

Labeling arises from interpreting evidence as permanent and external rather than temporary and external. Using the before mentioned example, being tired or not feeling well are both temporary, external factors. They are not related to the personality or character of the person in question ('external'), but rather a transient factor moderating their behavior ('temporary').

Labeling interacts with negative thinking, because negative thinkers often label themselves in negative ways. A negative thinker who fails a test may interpret themselves as stupid, rather than realizing that they were distracted during the test or that they didn't study enough.

The result is that problems or events that should be seen as changeable or small seem to be damming about their character. If you don't study hard enough for a test, for example, this can be improved by studying harder or more efficiently in the future. If you interpret yourself as stupid or dull however, this implies a problem that cannot necessarily be solved (hence leading to more negative states of mind and negative thinking patterns).

Therefore whenever you label yourself or others in future, negative thinker or not, consider the temporary-permanent and internal-external dimensions of labeling. When consciously considered, it is likely you will see that many behaviors and attributes you perceive are in fact temporary and external, rather than permanent and internal.

FILTERING

Filtering is the term applied to thinking patterns where a person focuses purely on the negative aspects of the situation. People who filter their thoughts might focus excessively on the one negative aspect of an otherwise pleasant experience and always extinguish positive thoughts with a greater, negative thought. For example, a person who filters might dwell on the fact that they made a bad first impression with someone they hadn't met before, ignoring the fact that the rest of their day was fantastic.

EMOTIONAL REASONING

This thought pattern is the tendency to believe that negative emotions felt reflect the reality of a situation. For example if someone feels as if they are stupid in a situation, they will believe that other people will interpret them as stupid, regardless of their actual displays of intelligence and competence.

MIND READING

This thought pattern refers to the tendency to presume that you know or understand what another person is thinking. In terms of negative thinking, this usually entails the presumption that other people are holding a negative perception of you or your actions.

Often, this perception is faulty. People who are 'mind readers' have a habit of picking up on minor or ambiguous body cues and believing that these cues are relevant to them. So for example, a person with mind reading thought habits might perceive a yawn as a sign of disinterest in their topic of conversion (therefore reducing their self-confidence) when it is actually just an indicator that the other person is sleep deprived.

MAGNIFICATION/MINIMIZATION

Magnification and minimization is the thought habit of exaggerating negative thoughts and under emphasizing negative thoughts respectively. When a person magnifies, they may perceive a trivial problem or occurrence as a full blown tragedy and when they minimize they may discredit or ignore their own success or achievements.

Depressed people have a tendency of showing an inverse pattern in regards to other people. To clarify, depressed people often magnify the success of other people and minimize their failures. The result is a comparatively skewed perception of themselves against other people, which likely both a cause and symptom of depression.

PERSONALIZATION

Personalization is the tendency to take blame and guilt for a circumstance or an event that is beyond control. For example if a conversation runs dry, as conversations occasionally do, a negative thinker might attribute this to themselves. This person might think that they are boring or have no social skills due to the conversation ending.

Similarly, if an accident happens at home and a family member injures themselves, a negative thinker who personalizes event might believe that the accident is their fault and that they could have prevented it, had they been there.

BLAMING

Conversely, instead of taking the responsibility upon themselves, you might have a tendency to blame others for negative circumstances. Blaming others can generate ill-will towards the people around you, but it can also induce a sense of helplessness and lack of control. If someone else is the cause of negative things or feelings that happen to you, than your ability to manage these feelings or events is limited. However, accepting appropriate blame or responsibility empowers yourself to make a positive change, when appropriate.

Blaming is often attributed to how a person *feels.* To clarify, you might blame someone for the fact that you are angry or sad, rather than blaming someone for breaking a glass or such. Blaming often is associated with thinking that the emotional state you feel is either deliberately and intentionally caused by the people around you, or caused by some degree of negligence. You might interpret that others have a responsibility to ensure you feel a certain way, and that your negative emotional state is due to a lack of required attention.

Realize that interpersonal relationships are complicated. Many slights and mishaps between people are purely unintentional. Furthermore, as a person you need to accept a large degree of ownership of your own emotions. Others can influence how you feel, but ultimately, only you can actually control your response to an event.

Mindfulness & Meditation

Now that you are aware of some of the negative thinking patterns you might be displaying, the next step in combating these patterns is being mindful. Life is taxing and distracting and many of us fall into the trap of acting and thinking on 'autopilot'.

We fail to consciously consider and interpret our actions or thoughts, which can lead to a variety of problems. In the case of negative thinkers, a lack of mindfulness means that their negative thoughts go unchallenged and therefore persist. Increasing your mindfulness allows you to apply the knowledge in the previous subsections when you recognize your thought patterns are negative.

One popular method to increase mindfulness is mindfulness meditation. Although there are several potential objects of this meditation, the most commonly used is the breath. Unlike the deep breathing technique mentioned earlier, a breathing meditation relies on observing the breath, rather than controlling it.

To start a breathing meditation, ensure that you have at least 15 minutes of time where you know you will not be interrupted. Likewise, reduce and eliminate ambient noise by turning off electrical devices and removing objects that produce noise.

For meditation it is best if you either sit in a chair or sit in a half lotus position (a type of cross-legged position where one foot rests on the opposite thigh and the other foot rests on the floor). Lying down tends to promote a certain degree of sleepiness, counteracting the very purpose of mindfulness meditation.

With all the preparations established, start to focus upon the breath. As before mentioned, you do not want to exhibit deliberate control of the breathing, rather you should attempt to focus upon the natural and unaided breathing pattern.

If you become distracted by thoughts (which you almost certainly will) bring your attention back to your natural breathing pattern. When you first start to meditate, it is likely that you will realize just how busy and distracted your mind actually is; many people find that they can barely focus upon the breath at all before they become distracted by a thought that pops into their head.

This is normal. Do not be discouraged or disheartened if this happens to you. Rather, gently and calmly bring your attention back towards the breath. It is important to be non-judgmental and display equanimity; do not chide yourself or be angry with yourself when your mind wanders. Instead, just focus once more, without any kind of mental commentary. Over time, you will be able to focus upon the breath with a deeper focus and experience fewer interruptions from wayward thoughts. Congratulations – your mindfulness is developing!

As a beginner to mindfulness meditation, there is no need to practice for more than 15 minutes a day. For most novices, anything more than this can feel rather overwhelming and it can be uncomfortable to sit for longer periods of time.

However, as you continue to meditate, you may wish to gradually extend your meditation sessions. It is not unheard of for advanced meditation practitioners to meditate for hours at a time, but the majority of people find that a period of 30-45 minutes produces a noticeable change in mindfulness (as well as a greater amount of inner peace, relaxation and other mental benefits).

When persistently practiced mindfulness meditation should help you be more alert and more aware during your day-to-day life. This in turn should help you recognize your current thought patterns, allowing you to shy away from negative thought patterns altogether.

Mindfulness can also be cultivated by trying to be mindful during everyday tasks. It is easy to go into an autopilot mode during repetitive or dull activities we do every day – such as our work, cleaning, cooking, eating, walking, etc.

Instead of allowing your mind to wander during these activities, try to engage with them on a more intimate level. Feel all the physical sensations of your muscles as you wash and clean and perform that activity to the best of your ability – focusing on all the grime and dirt you intend to remove. When you walk somewhere, be aware of the pace and feel of the walk as well as the sounds, scents and feelings of the world around you.

This greater level of mindfulness has two benefits. Firstly, being mindful of everyday action gives your mind less space and opportunity to drift into negative thinking territories. Instead of dwelling on yesterday's problems or tomorrow's you simply focus on what is happening at this very moment in time.

Likewise, being present in the current moment may have uplifting qualities of its own accord. Mindfulness is increasingly being sought as a method for eliminating depression and its positive effects are well documented.

CONCLUSION

Mental health isn't something you should ignore. If you are feeling stressed, anxious or you are aware that your negative thought patterns are detrimental to your life, you need to take action. For most of us, it only takes a small amount of knowledge and discipline to apply a few techniques that can drastically improve our state of mind.

This book has provided you with an assortment of those techniques. In the first chapter you learned about stress and its definition as the sensation of being overwhelmed by pressure and responsibilities. You were taught about the fight or flight response and stressors, both physiological and psychological. Lastly you learned techniques to limit your exposure to stressors and change your perception of them.

In the second chapter, you were given a run-down of anxiety from a psychological perspective. You were told about the importance of a healthy lifestyle and given tutelage in various relaxation and anxiety management techniques, such as deep breathing and the anxiety period.

Finally, in the third chapter you tackle negative thinking. You learned how negative thinking arises from cognitive distortions and the various types of these distortions, such as 'all or nothing thinking' and labeling. Finally, you were taught how to cultivate mindfulness and recognize patterns of negative thinking, in order to change them.

Message from the Author

Thank you!

Please check out my author page on Amazon to see my latest publications. Please don't forget to download your Free Gift!

Once again I want to thank you for reading my book. I really hope you got a lot out of it.

If you enjoyed this book I would really appreciate it if you could leave me a positive review on Amazon. You can click here to go directly to the book on Amazon and leave your review.

I love getting feedback from my readers and reviews on Amazon really do make a difference. I read all my reviews and would really appreciate your thoughts.

Thanks so much.

Scott Colter

FREE GIFT

Drop the Fat Now!
Natural Solutions to Getting Trim

>>Click Here To Download "Drop the Fat Now" for FREE<<